'50s TV Lamps

Calvin Shepherd

Schiffer Publishing Ltd

4880 Lower Valley Rd. Atglen, PA 19310 USA

Dedication

To my wife of forty-four years, Joyce Self Shepherd. Without her love for antiques and collectibles this book would not have been possible. She has traveled several hundred miles with me only to purchase one TV lamp. Thank you "Mi Honi."

Copyright © 1998 by Calvin Shepherd
Library of Congress Catalog Card Number: 98-84848

Designed by Bonnie M. Hensley
Layout by Randy L. Hensley
Typeset in Impress BT/Aldine 721

ISBN: 0-7643-0601-4
Printed in China
1 2 3 4

Published by Schiffer Publishing Ltd.
4880 Lower Valley Road Atglen, PA 19310
Phone: (610) 593-1777; Fax: (610) 593-2002
E-mail: Schifferbk@aol.com

In Europe Schiffer books are distributed by
Bushwood Books 6 Marksbury Avenue
Kew Gardens Surrey TW9 4JF England
Phone: 44 (0) 181 392-8585; Fax: 44 (0) 181 392-9876
E-mail: Bushwd@aol.com

Please write for a free catalog.
This book may be purchased from the publisher.
Please include $3.95 for shipping. Please try your bookstore first.

We are interested in hearing from authors
with book ideas on related subjects.

Table of Contents

Acknowledgments

My sincere thanks to the following people who contributed to the production of this book. First a wonderful lady and friend, Kay Martin of Visalia, California. Kay allowed me to come into her home and photograph her beautiful lamps. Also my thanks to Greg Crass of Kingsburg, California, for his terrific photography skills.

Others who have helped me with my collection of TV lamps are Steve and La Nora Shepherd, Rodney Shepherd, Linda Griffis, Mike and Kathy Edwards, Larry and Diane Marshall, Mildred Bethel, Shirley Green and Karen Grilione of G & G Liquidation, Judy Jiminez of Auburn, California, Barbara Allen and Regina Almeida of Phoenix, Arizona, Jeri Spradley of The Country Depot in Fresno, California, Rich and Pat White of Whites House Mall in Visalia, California, Marion and Bob Johnson of Clovis Antique Mall, Stores 1 and 2, in Clovis, California, Mary Jane McKinsey of Antique Mall of Clinton, Oklahoma, and Bette Haynes and Janice Arnett of Recollections Antiques & Collectables in Oakdale, California. And my mother, Mrs. Rosie Shepherd, of Selma, California. To anyone that I may have missed, thank you.

Introduction

When mass production of the newly invented televisions began in the early 1950s, indirect lighting was needed to improve viewing quality. Thus the TV lamp was introduced to meet this requirement. The uniquely designed and decorative TV lamps served a useful purpose, to preserve eyesight. It was feared that the small screens and unclear pictures on these televisions would cause people to go blind unless they used "back-light." The TV lamp was also produced to decorate and enhance the beauty of the new line of televisions being manufactured by Motorola, Zenith, and Philco

The TV lamps were produced in a wide variety of styles and colors. Most were made of high-gloss ceramics. These were glazed and painted in popular 1950s colors like green (chartreuse), maroon, white, black, and pink. The illumination in most of the lamps came from a single bulb in the back of the figure known as a "back-light."

Other lamps with the bulb inside would create an "up-light" effect. The figures most often represented in TV lamps were siamese cats, panthers, dogs, mallards, ducks, swans, and ships. Some TV lamps also served other functions, doubling as planters, candy dishes, or clocks.

The TV lamp was very popular in the '50s because of its beauty and usefulness. However, when television viewing quality improved, along with changes in cabinet design the TV lamp lost its place in the American home. Popular for less than ten years, TV lamps were packed away in closets and attics and forgotten.

The TV lamps from the 1950s are now reemerging from storage and finding their way to garage sales, flea markets, and antique shops. Prices for TV lamps range from $10 to several hundred.

The most popular and distinct lamps were made by Lane and Co. of Van Nuys of California, Maddux of Los Angeles, California; Haeger Potteries of Dundee, Illinois; McCoy Pottery of Zanesville, Ohio, and Kron of Bangs, Texas. Other lesser-known companies made some choice lamps. Some ceramic companies made TV lamps to be used as promotional items. The lamps were given to customers when they purchased new television sets. These lamps were sometimes called salesman samples.

The prices given for TV lamps in this book assume that they are in excellent condition, with no chips or cracks. The wiring in most cases has been replaced for safety purposes. The prices are based on my observations on the West Coast. Prices in the central and eastern United States may vary.

Chapter 1
Dogs and Cats

Pink poodle candy dish by Lane and Co. of Van Nuys, California, 13" tall,; $150.

Pug and poodle by Kron of Texas, 13" tall, $125.

Basset hound, painted plaster, 9" tall, $45.

Basset hound by Maddux of California, 11.5" tall, $65.

Cocker spaniel puppies, Claes copyright U.S.A., 8.25" tall, $55.

Boxer by Royal of California,
15" tall, $70.

Pointer, 14" long, $65.

Boxers, Claes copyright 1956, 13" tall, $85.

Poodle planter by Royal of California, 15" long, $55.

Scottie puppies, 8.5" tall, $65.

Toy poodle planter, 13" long, $50.

Brown toy poodle, 10.5" tall, $60.

Racing grey hounds, 9" tall, $60.

Siamese cats by Kron of Texas, 13.5" tall, $140.

Siamese cats, Claes copyright 1959, 11" tall, $60.

Siamese cats, black and cream, Claes copyright 1954, 12" tall, $50.

Siamese cats, black and white, Claes copyright 1954, 12" tall, $50.

Kittens in a basket, 8"
tall, $55.

Siamese cat family by Lane and Co. of Van Nuys, California, 12.5" tall, $75.

Siamese Cats, black and white, by Lane and Co. of Van Nuys, California, 12" tall, $45.

Siamese Cats, white and brown, by Lane and Co. of Van Nuys, California, 12" tall, $65.

Siamese cat family, made in California, 11.5" tall, $65.

Siamese Cats, made in California 12" tall, $45.

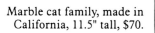

Marble cat family, made in California, 11.5" tall, $70.

Chapter 2
Panthers

Panther candy dish, 14" long, $65.

Black panther, 9" tall, $55.

Striped tiger, Modernera Lamp of Los Angeles, 7.5" tall, $55.

Panther with gold stripes, adjustable metal lamp, 15" long, $65.

Panther planter by Kron of Texas, 15" long, $80.

Panther planter by Lane and Co. of Van Nuys, California, 15" long, $80.

Chartreuse panther by Lane and Co. of Van Nuys, California, 15" long, $85.

Panther by Lane and Co. of Van Nuys, California, 9.5" tall, $75.

Dark green panther by Lane and Co. of Van Nuys, California, 15" long, $75.

White panther by Kron of Texas, 16.5" long, $95.

Striped tiger, 14.5"
long, $55.

Black panther by Kron of Texas, 11.5" long, $55.

Black panther, 6.5" tall, $45.

Brown panther by Kron of Bangs,
Texas, 9" tall, $55.

Black panther, 9" tall, $50.

Fighting panthers, 12" tall, $75.

Brown panther by Kron of Texas, 7.5" tall, $55.

Chartreuse panther by Lane and Co. of Van Nuys, California, 20" long, $65.

Black panther, 11" long, $55.

Green panther, 21" long, $60.

Panther by Jucqulig Lamp Co., 23" long, $65.

Panther by La Miane China, 21" long, $75.

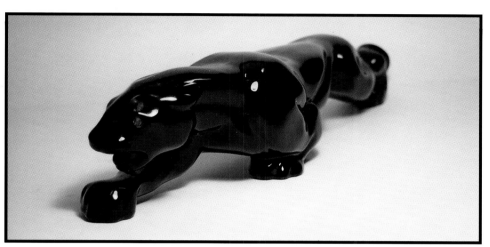

Black panther, 19" long, $60.

Panther with yellow eyes, 23" long, $65.

Black panther with red eyes, 22" long, $65.

Maroon panther, 20" long, $70.

Panther with red eyes, 19.5" long, $65.

Panther by Royal China and Novelty Co., 1953, 20.5" long, $75.

Panther with green eyes, 20.5" long, $55.

Panther, 21" long, $70.

Panther, 14" long, $45.

Panther, chartreuse green, 6.5" tall, $40.

Panther planter with fiberglass shade,
8.5" tall, $40.

Black panther, 6.5" tall, $40.

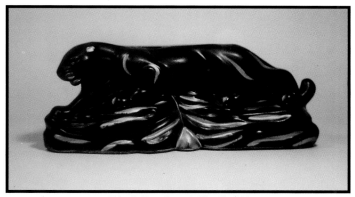

Black Panther, 4.5" tall, $40.

Maroon panther, 6.5" tall, $40.

Green panther, 11" long, $40.

Panther planter by Hollywood Ceramics, 8.5" tall, $50.

Green panther, 7" tall, $45.

Panther, 9.5" tall, $40.

Black panther by Lane and Co. of Van Nuys, California, 1956, 12" tall, $90.

Black Panther by Lane and Co. of Van Nuys,
California, 10.5" tall, $80.

Chapter 3

Horses

Horse candy dish by Lane and Co. of Van Nuys, California, 11.5" tall, $85.

Horse candy dish by Lane and Co. of Van Nuys, California, 13.5"
tall, $80.

Horse candy dish by Lane and Co. of Van Nuys, California, 14" tall, $90.

Horse head, 8" tall, $50.

Horse planter by Lane and Co. of Van Nuys, California, 9.25" tall, $90.

Horse head, 9.5" tall, $60.

Horse head, 8" tall, $50.

Horse head by Kron of Texas, 11" tall, $125.

Black horse head, 8" tall, $50.

Brown horse head, 8" tall, $50.

Horse head by Kron of Texas, 16" long, $100.

Horse head with colt, made in U.S.A., 11.5" tall, $75.

Horse head, 10"
tall, $55.

Rearing horse, 14.5" tall, $55.

Horse head with colt, made in California, 11.5" tall, $65.

Fighting stallions, 13"
tall, $70.

31

Brown horse with colt, 8.5" tall, $40.

Black horse with colt, 8.5" tall, $40.

White horse with colt, 8.5" tall, $40.

Dark green horse, 9" tall, $45.

Horse planter, 10.5" tall, $40.

Horse planter, 10.5" tall, $40.

Brown horse by Lane and Co. of Van Nuys, California, 11" tall, $65.

Dark brown horse Lane and Co. of Van Nuys,
California, 13" tall, $65.

Palomino horse by
Maddux of California,
12.5" tall, $65.

Brown horse by Maddux of California, 12.5" tall, $65.

White horse by Maddux of California, 12.5" tall, $65.

Horse of painted plaster, 12.5" tall, $60.

White horse with colt, 11" tall, $55.

Horse planter, made in U.S.A., 9" tall, $50.

Horse, bright orange, 11.5" tall, $55.

Bronze carnival horse, 11.5" tall, $45.

Black horse, 10" tall, $55.

Brown horse with fiberglass back shade, 9.5" tall, $60.

Black horse planter, 11" tall, $55.

Parade horse, 12" tall, $65.

Palomino horse, 10.5" tall, $50.

Horse planter by Royal Haeger, 11" tall, $55.

Green horse, 10.5" tall, $50.

Lady rider shooting deer, 10" tall, $85.

Pink horse planter by Gilner, 10" tall, $45.

Green horse planter by Gilner, 10" tall, $45.

Horse planter by Gilner, 10" tall, $45.

Cowboy on bronco with glass back shade, 12" tall, $55.

Fighting horse planter, American China, 8" tall, $55.

Horse planter by Maddux of California, $65.

Horse head vase, 8" tall, $40.

Horse head planter, 5" tall, $35.

Pony, 11.5" tall, $40.

Horse, 8.5" tall, $40.

Horse planter, 8.5" tall, $40.

Black horse, 13" tall, $65.

Chapter 4

Other Animals and Fish

Fawn candy dish by Lane and Co. of Van Nuys, California, 1959, $65.

Deer with fawn, 15" tall, $40.

Big horn sheep planter, 8" tall, $40.

Deer planter, 10" tall, $45.

Deer by Maddux of California,
11.5" tall, $65.

Deer planter, 10" tall, $40.

Deer head planter by Gilner Co., 13" tall, $50.

Big horn sheep, 10" tall, $45.

Deer with fawn, 10" tall, $45.

Deer by Genie Ceramics of
Lynwood, California, 10" tall, $55.

Deer planter by Kron of Texas, 11" tall, $60.

Ram planter by Cali-Co of California, 13" long, 1953, $50.

Big horn sheep, 9.5" tall, $45.

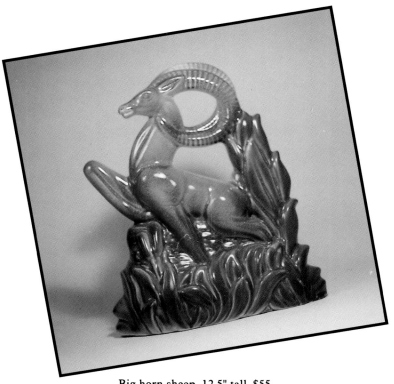

Big horn sheep, 12.5" tall, $55.

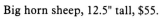

Deer head planter, 9.5" tall, $40.

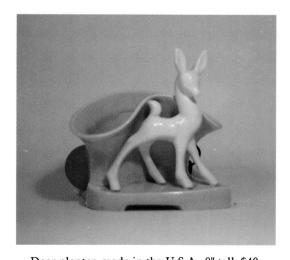

Deer planter, made in the U.S.A., 8" tall, $40.

Deer, 10.5" tall, $45.

45

Deer planter, 10" long, $35.

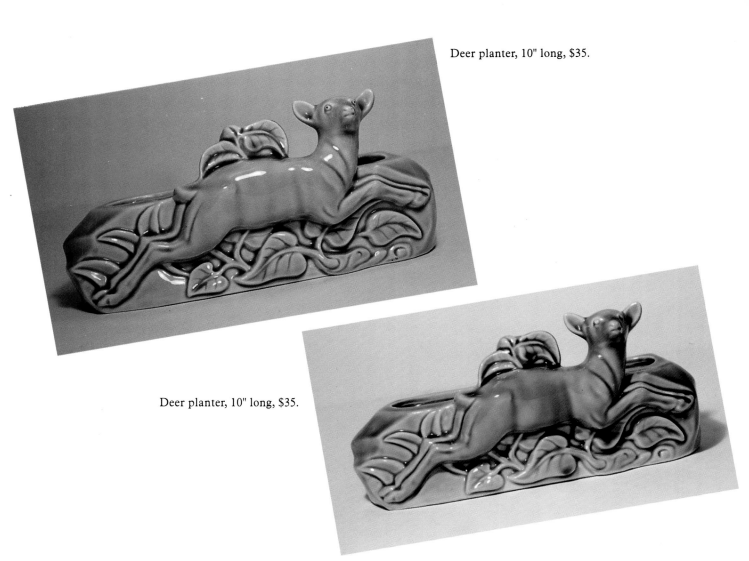

Deer planter, 10" long, $35.

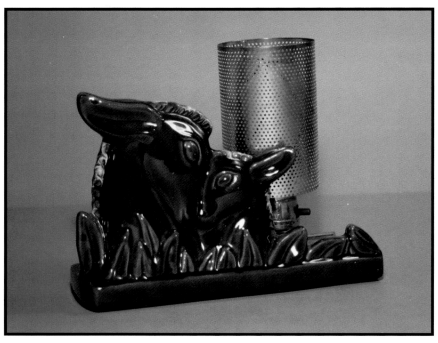

Deer with fawn, 7.5" tall, $50.

Zebra TV lamp, 12" long, $40.

Unicorn, 14.5" tall, $55.

Elephant, 6.5" tall, $45.

Green bull, 9.5" tall, $50.

Rabbit, 8" tall, $40.

Black bull by Maddux of California, #859, 11.5" tall, $60.

Sail fish candy dish by Lane and Co. of Van Nuys, California, 14" tall, $95.

Fish planter by Hollywood Ceramics, 9.5" tall, $50.

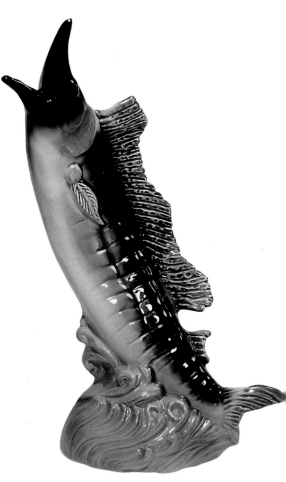

Fish, 15.5" tall, $60.

Fish school, 13" tall, $45.

Fish planter from C. Miller Co., 1956, 21" long, $50.

Fish, 16" long, $55.

Swordfish, 10.5" long, $45.

Swordfish, 10.5" long, $45.

Fish planter 10.5" long, $45.

Fish planter, 10.5" long, $45.

Swordfish, 9" tall, $50.

Dolphin Trio by Enchanto of California, 12" tall, $60.

Fish planter by Cali-Co of California, 9" tall, $50.

Chapter 5

Ducks and Swans

Duck family by Lane and Co. of Van Nuys, California, $65.

Mallard duck planter by Lane and Co. of Van Nuys, California, 1954-1958, 13" tall, $75.

Mallard duck by Maddux of California, 11.5" tall, $60.

Mallard duck, 12.5" tall, $55.

Mallard duck with gold trim by Lane and Co. of Van Nuys, California, 1954-1956, 14" tall, $85.

Mallard duck by Maddux of California, 11" tall, $70.

Ducks, painted plaster, 11.5" tall, $60.

Mallard duck planter, 10.5" tall, $65.

Duck planter, 16" long, $55.

Mallard duck, 11" tall, $45.

Duck planter by Hollywood Ceramics, 7.5" tall, $45.

Duck planter by Hollywood Ceramics, 7.5" tall, $45.

Swan by Maddux of California, 9.75" tall, $75.

Swan planter by Maddux of California, 10" tall, $70.

Swan, made in the U.S.A., 10" tall, $65.

Swan planter by Royal Fleet of California, 9" tall, $50.

Swan planter by Royal Fleet of California, 9" tall, $50.

Swan planter by Royal Fleet of California, 9" tall, $50.

Swan planter, 10" tall, $55.

White swan with blue base by Maddux of California, 12" tall, $55.

White swan by Maddux of California, 12" tall, $55.

Swan planter, made in the U.S.A., 9.5" tall, $60.

Swan, 9" tall, $50.

Swan, 9.5" tall, $45.

Swan, Made by Donna, 9.5" tall, $40.

Swan, 1950, 8" tall, $40.

Swan 9" tall, $45.

Swan TV lamp, 8" tall, $40.

Green swan, 11" tall, $60.

Swan, 9" tall, $55.

Swan, 8.5" tall, $40.

Swan, black marble, 12" tall, $55.

Swan, green and white, 12" tall, $55.

Swan planter, 8.5" tall, $35.

Chapter 6

Roosters and Other Birds

Rooster by Lane and Co. of Van Nuys, California, 15" tall, $70.

Rooster by Lane and Co. of Van Nuys, California, 15" tall, $65.

Rooster by Lane and Co. of Van Nuys, California, 13" tall, $70.

Rooster by Lane and Co. of Van Nuys, California, . 15" tall, $70.

Rooster, 12" tall, $55.

Rooster by Lane and Co. of Van Nuys, California, 12.5" tall, $65.

Fighting rooster, 11" tall, $55.

Rooster, chalkware by Maddux of California, 10" tall, $60.

Rooster, 11.5" tall, $50.

Rooster, 11.5" tall, $50.

Rooster, 11.5" tall, $50.

Rooster, 11.5" tall, $50.

Rooster, 7.5" tall, $40.

Flamingo candy dish by Lane and Co. of Van Nuys, California, 1957, 14" tall, $350.

Owl by Kron of Bangs, Texas, 11.5" tall, $100.

Owl by Maddux of California, 1970, 12" tall, $75.

Pheasant, 12.5" tall, $55.

Black Bird by Kron of Texas, 17.5" tall, $70.

Crane in flight by California Original, $75.

Roadrunner by Maddux of California, 9.5" tall, $70.

White pheasant, made in the U.S.A., 11.5" tall, $50.

Peacock Planter by Royal Fleet of California, 10" tall, $55.

Pink pheasant, made in the U.S.A., 11.5" tall, $50.

Parakeets, 8" tall, $45.

Red bird planter by Hollywood Creation, 6" tall, $45.

Yellow bird planter, 8.5" tall, $35.

Brown parrots, Holland Mold, 10" tall, $50.

Painted Parrots, Holland Mold, 10" tall, $55.

Flamingo planter by La Velle of California,
9.5" tall, $45.

71

Pea fowl by Royal Fleet of California, 10" tall, $50.

Pea fowl by Royal Fleet of California, $50.

Pea fowl by Royal Fleet of California, 10" tall, $50.

Pea fowl by Royal Fleet of California, 10" tall, $50.

Chapter 7
Boats, Wagons, and Cars

Sailboat, 14" long, $50.

Sailboat, painted plaster by Garland Creations, 13.5" tall, $50.

Sailboat 10" tall, $45.

Pirate ship, painted plaster, 16.5" tall, $55.

Sailboat in 1950s green and gold, 10" tall, $60.

Sailboat by Marria of California, 9.5" tall, $60.

Sailboat, 13.5" tall, $45.

Paddleboat, 14.5" long, $45.

Paddleboat, 14.5" long, $45.

Sailboat, solid bronze, 13" tall, $50.

Sailboat, 11.5" tall, $40.

Sailboat with gold sails, 10.5" long, $40.

Sailboat with stainless sails, 14" tall, $55.

Sailboat, 13.5" tall, $45.

Sailboat with stainless sails, 14" tall, $55.

Sailboat, 13.5" long, $45.

Sailboat with iridescent color and stainless sails, 13" tall, $65.

Sailboat, 10.5" tall, $40.

Sailboat, 10.5" tall, $40.

Sailboat, 9" tall, $40.

Sailboat, 9" tall, $40.

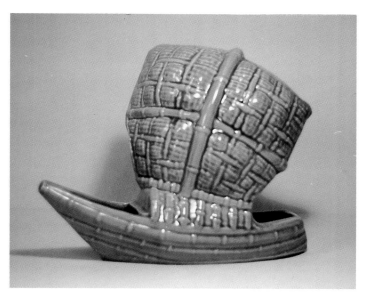

Boat with bamboo sails by Comer Creation, 10" tall, $35.

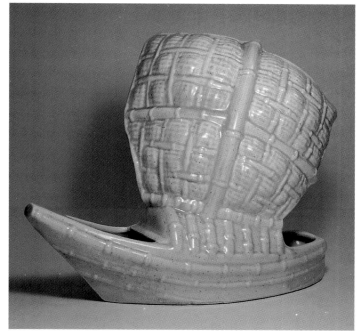

Sailboat by Comer Creation, 10" tall, $35.

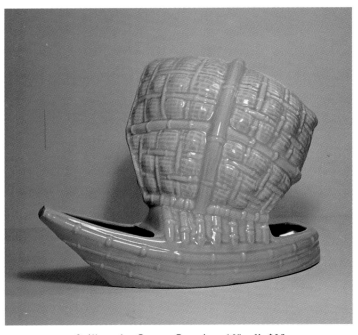

Sailboat by Comer Creation, 10" tall, $35.

Sailboat by Comer Creation, 10" tall, $35.

Sailboat by Comer Creation, 10" tall, $35.

Boat planter, 8.5" tall, $35.

Covered wagon (cover not original), 11" long, $45.

Covered wagon, 10" long, $45.

Covered wagon with cork wheels and frame, 12" long, $45.

Covered wagon by Marcia of
California, 11" long, $55.

Covered wagon with oxen of painted plaster, 14" long, $60.

Covered wagon with oxen, 15" long, $60.

Covered wagon, 8" long, $40.

Covered Wagon by Maddux of California, 8" tall, $50.

Covered wagon, 7" tall, $45.

Stage coach, 6" tall, $40.

Stage coach with metal wheels and rack, 8" tall, $50.

Stage coach, 6" tall, $40.

Stage coach, 6" tall, $40.

Early convertible by Buckingham Ceramics, 5.5" tall, $45.

Early convertible by Buckingham Ceramics, 5.5" tall, $45.

Early convertible by Buckingham Ceramics, 5.5" tall, $45.

Chapter 8

People and Faces

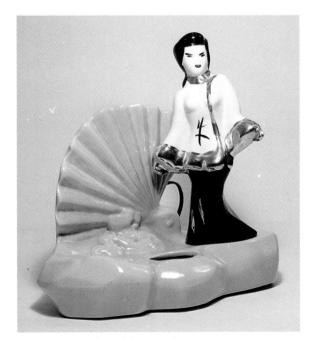

Oriental lady, 11.5" tall, $50.

Egyptian lady with gold panther, 13" tall, $85.

Colonial couple candy dish,
12.5" tall, $85.

Matador by Lane and Co. of Van Nuys, California, 16" tall, $65.

Matador by Lane and Co. of Van Nuys, California, 15.5" tall, $90.

African dancers, 10" tall, $60.

88

Lady head, Navis and Smith Co., Chicago, Illinois, 12" tall, $80.

Black head, 12.5" tall, $90.

Egyptian head,
10.5" tall, $45.

Lady head, Navis and Smith Co., Chicago, Illinois, 12" tall, $80.

Toby Mug by Sawage of California, 9" tall, $100.

Toby Mug by Sawage of California, 9" tall, $100.

Chinese couple on junk by Premco Mfg. Co. of Chicago, Illinois, 1954, 15" long, $55.

Chinese couple on junk by Premco Mfg. Co. of Chicago, Illinois, 1954, $55.

Chinese couple on a jumk by Fuhry and Sons of Cleveland, Ohio, 16.5" long, $85.

Chinese couple by Fuhry and Sons of Cleveland, Ohio, 1954, 10" tall, $55.

Oriental couple, painted plaster by Silvestri Bros., 9.5" tall, $65.

Oriental couple with fiberglass shades, 10" tall, $45.

Mermaid on a shell, Cali-Co of California, 8.5" tall, $45.

Mermaid on a shell by Cali-Co of California, 8.5" tall, $45.

Mermaid on a shell, Comer Creations, 8.5" tall, $40.

Mermaid on a shell, Comer Creations, 8.5" tall, $40.

Mermaid planter, Comer Creations, 8.5" tall, $40.

Couple on a carousel, 7.5" tall, $35.

Comedy and tragedy masks by Royal Haeger of
California, 9.5" tall, $50.

Comedy and tragedy masks by Tri-Wonder Lamp of Madison, Wisconsin, 8" tall, $50.

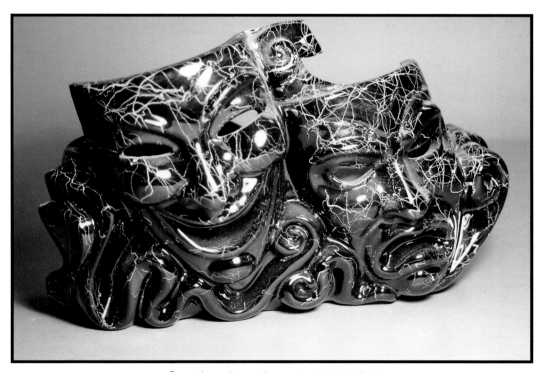

Comedy and tragedy masks, 8.5" tall, $45.

Chapter 9

Vases and Fans

Art Deco TV lamp, brass with alabaster shade, 14" tall, $300.

White fan with a gold rose, 10" tall, $60.

Fan, 8.5" tall, $45.

Fan with 22-Karat gold trim, La Velle of California, 9.5" tall, $50.

Fan with 22-Karat gold trim, La Velle of California, 9.5" tall, $50.

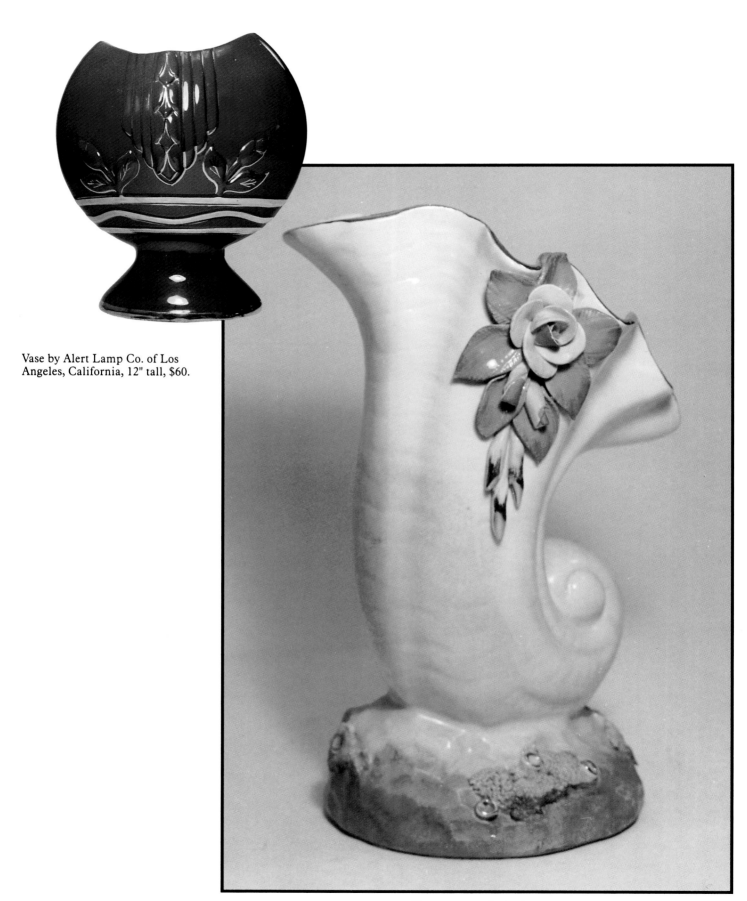

Vase by Alert Lamp Co. of Los
Angeles, California, 12" tall, $60.

Horn vase, 11.5" tall, $50.

Vase, 8.5" tall, $45.

Vase, 7.5" tall, $30.

Vase, hand painted, 10" tall, $60.

Vase, Crenshaw No. C-401, 8.5" tall, $40.

Vase, 8" tall, $35.

Kerosene lamp by Kleine Co., 8" tall, $50.

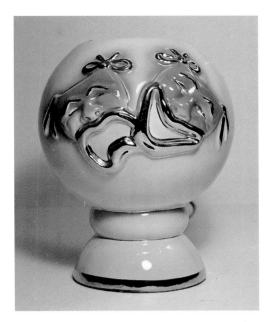

Comedy and tragedy masks globe, 9.25" tall, $55.

Vase, 8" tall, $35.

Vase with Oriental painting, 7" tall, $30.

Planter by Le Ann of California, 9" tall, $45.

Vase, 8.5" tall, $50.

103

Vase, 9.5" tall, $40.

Vase, 9.5" tall, $40.

Vase with dragon design by Walco TV
Lamp 10" tall, $60.

Vase with dragon design by Walco TV Lamp, 10" tall, $60.

Vase by Royal Haeger of California, 7.5" tall, $40.

Vase by Royal Haeger of California, 7.5" tall, $40.

Vase by Royal Haeger of California, 7.5" tall, $40.

Tulip vase by Ceramic
Arts of California, 9.5"
tall, $50.

Tulip vase by Esco-lite, 9" tall, $45.

Tulip base by Ceramic Arts of California, 9.5" tall, $50.

Tulip vase by Esco-lite, 9" tall, $45.

Tulip vase by Esco-lite, 9" tall, $45.

Tulip vase by Esco-lite, 9" tall, $45.

Tulip vase by Esco-lite, 9" tall, $45.

Chapter 10

Planters

Sunflower planter, 8.5" tall, $30.

Leaf planter, 8" tall, $35.

Leaf planter with fiberglass back shade, 8" tall, $40.

Leaf planter with fiberglass back shade, 8" tall, $40.

Ivy leaf planter, 8" tall, $35.

Planter with metal stand, 7" tall, $40.

Planter by Sierra-Columbia of
Pasadena, California, $30.

Planter, U.S.A. California
Original, 6" tall, $40.

Planter, by Maddux of California, 7.5" tall, $40.

Planter by Sierra-Columbia of Pasadena, California, 5.5" tall, $30.

Planter by Sierra-Columbia of Pasadena, California, 5.5" tall, $30.

Planter by Sierra-Columbia of Los Angeles, California, 6" tall, $35.

Planter by Sierra-Columbia of Los Angeles, California, 6" tall, $30.

Planter by Sierra-Columbia of Pasadena, California, 5.5" tall, $30.

Planter, by Maddux of California, 6" tall, $35.

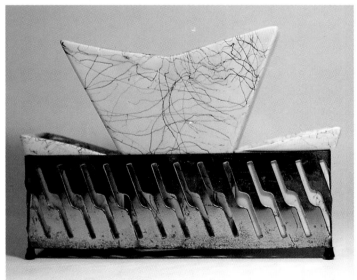

Planter, 8" tall, $30.

Planter, Made in U.S.A.
1955 5.5" tall, $35.

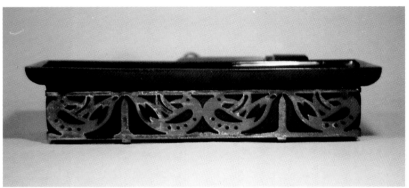

Planter by Northington, 15" long, $40.

Planter, 3.5" tall, $25.

Planter by Maddux of California, 6" tall, $30.

Planter by Castro Mfg. of Hollywood, 6" tall, $45.

Planter by Wayne of Hollywood, 7" tall, $35.

Planter by Hollywood Ceramics, 6" tall, $40.

Leaf planter, 5.5" tall, $35.

Planter by Stewart B. McCullough, $45.

Planter, 5" tall, $25.

Planter, 5" tall, $35.

Miscellaneous Lamps

Shell, iridescent pearl, 7" tall, $45.

Shell by Maddux of California, 1962, 10" tall, $65.

Shell, 8" tall, $50.

Shell by Maddux of California, 10" tall, $60.

Ocean wave, Gidget Fair Stores, San Francisco, 7" tall, $35.

White cloud, 7.5" tall, $30.

Seashell, 7" tall, $30.

Wagon wheel, 11.5" tall, $45.

Oriental arbor by Schor-Par Craft of New York, 11" tall, $45.

Frogs on lily pad by Royal of California, 7" tall, $45.

Butterfly by SNAS of California, 9.5" tall, $50.

Shell beach screen, 7" tall, $35.

Fireplace by Marcia of California, 7" tall, $45.

Brown mill, 12" long, $45.

121

Pitcher, hand painted, 13" tall, $45.

Pitcher and bowl, 7" tall, $40.

Rear view of above lamp.

Brown glass candy dish, 7.5" tall, $30.

Lamp and candy dish, 7.5" tall, $30.

TV lamp, 8" tall, $40.

Modern art by Zill Hutchins of California, 10" tall, $45.

124

TV lamp, 9" tall, $45.

Leaf by Lanell of California, 9.5" tall, $45.

Leaf planter by Royal of California, 7" tall, $45.

Leaf planter by Royal of
California, 7" tall, $45.

Leaf by Marcia of California, 9" tall, $45.

Leaf, 8.5" tall, $30.

Leaf, 8.5" tall, $30.

Leaf, 8.5" tall, $30.

Leaf by Esco-lite of Los Angeles, 11" tall, $45.

Leaf by Esco-lite of Los Angeles, 11" tall, $45.

Leaf by Gilner, 9.5" tall, $40.

Leaf by Gilner, 9.5" tall, $40.

Leaf planter by Easher Co. of Los
Angeles, 11" tall, $45.

Leaf by Lane and Co. of Van Nuys, California, 1958, 14.5" tall, $60.

Clock by Stnola Lamps, 12"
tall, $40.